Drugs on the Street

Anne Rooney

TITLES IN THE VOICES SERIES:

AIDS • CHILD LABOUR • DRUGS ON THE STREET • GANGS •

HUNGER • POVERTY • RACE HATE • RELIGIOUS EXTREMISM

VIOLENCE • WAR

First published in paperback in 2010
by Evans Brothers Limited
2A Portman Mansions
Chiltern Street
London W1U 6NR

VISIT OUR WEBSITE www.evansbooks.co.uk

The right of Anne Rooney to be identified as the author of this Work has been asserted by her in accordance with the Copyright, Designs and Patents Act 1988.

British Library Cataloguing in Publication Data
Rooney, Anne
Drugs on the street. – (Voices)
1. Drug abuse – Juvenile literature
2. Drug abuse and crime – Juvenile literature
I. Title
364.1'77

ISBN 978 0 237 54216 0

Editor: Susie Brooks
Designer: Mayer Media Ltd
Picture research: Sally Cole and Lynda Lines

Produced for Evans Brothers Limited by
Monkey Puzzle Media Limited
48 York Avenue
Hove, BN3 1PJ

Picture acknowledgements
Photographs were kindly supplied by the following: Corbis 11 (Peter Turnley), 28 (Brenda Ann Kenneally); Getty Images front cover (Stewart Bonney News Agency), 17 (Richard Radstone), 19 (Karen Moskowitz), 24 (BP), 30, 31, 35 (Stewart Bonney News Agency), 41 (Larry Dale Gordon); Photofusion 22 (Simon de Trey-White); Reuters 4 (Dan Chung), 16 (Asim Tanveer), 21 (John Schults), 29, 33 (Stephen Hird), 36 (Will Burgess), 43; Rex Features 1 (Alex Adams), 6 (Image Source), 12, 13 (SIPA), 14 (John Powell), 15 (Alex Adams), 18 (Phanie Agency), 26 (John Powell), 27, 32 (Richard Gardner), 34 (Sakki), 44–45 (John Powell); Still Pictures 20 (Hartmut Schwarzbach); Topfoto.co.uk 5 (Teake Zuidema/The Image Works), 7 (John Powell), 8 (Tony Savino/The Image Works), 9 (ArenaPAL), 10, 23, 25, 37, 38, 39 (Zoriah/The Image Works), 40, 42 (Larry Mulvehill/The Image Works).

CONTENTS

WHAT ARE DRUGS?

People have been using drugs of different kinds for thousands of years – to relax, to distract themselves from hardship and misery, or to encourage mystical or religious visions. But what are drugs?

Many kinds

Drugs can be anything people take to alter their mental state. They range from 'hard' drugs, such as cocaine, to the solvents in aerosols, legal drugs such as alcohol and tobacco, and medicines either prescribed by doctors or taken without medical advice. This book concentrates on illegal street drugs.

Adrian, from Amsterdam in the Netherlands, explains how he tried all the drugs he could find:

❝ I went straight from pot to ecstasy without a thought. After I started on club drugs, I did anything I could get hold of. I did mushrooms, acid, nitrous oxide, speed, special K [ketamine], and cocaine. Everything – I tried everything. I was out to experiment. ❞

Many people enjoy occasional use of drugs, such as this woman smoking cannabis at the Glastonbury rock festival, UK.

When people can no longer control their use of drugs, they become addicts, like this man taking cocaine in Brazil.

Use or abuse?

Many people use drugs of one type or another. Many users try them for a while and then give up. But for some people, use turns into abuse when they are no longer in control or become dependent on the drugs. Drug abuse can have lasting physical and mental effects – it can even cause death. And drugs can be very difficult to give up.

Gaynor lives in Wisconsin in Canada. She explains how taking speed has affected her:

❝ Half an hour after taking it, the world was all mine. It was like nothing I had ever felt. I was full of energy, and confidence. I felt I could accomplish anything; I'd found ultimate happiness. That was 1995 – but I didn't have a clue. Ten years on I'm trapped in the reality of drugs. It seems like there's no way out. ❞

Sadly, the 'reality of drugs' for many people is despair, poverty and a compelling need to keep taking them.

DRUG USE AROUND THE WORLD

% OF TOTAL USERS IN DIFFERENT AREAS

DRUG	ESTIMATED TOTAL USERS	NORTH AMERICA	SOUTH AMERICA	WESTERN EUROPE	EASTERN EUROPE	OCEANIA	ASIA	AFRICA
CANNABIS	144.1 million	15%	10%	12%	3%	3%	37%	19%
AMPHETAMINES	24 million	58%*		14%	5%	3%	10%	11%
ECSTASY	4.5 million	27%	<1%	51%	7%	9%	4%	2%
COCAINE	14 million	50%	22%	16%	1%	1%	1%	9%
HEROIN	9.2 million	13%*		15%**		6%	61%	5%

(* North and South America combined   ** Western and Eastern Europe combined)
United Nations Drug Control Program, World Drug Report, 2001

WHY START TAKING DRUGS?

Everyone is told that drugs are dangerous – that they can cause lasting physical or mental damage or lead to addiction. So why do people start taking drugs?

Breaking away

Some people take drugs through boredom, or because they are looking for a way out of depression and misery. Others take drugs to make a statement. Charlotte, from southern England, tried heroin as an act of rebellion. She revels in doing something so forbidden:

❝ I wanted to break all the rules. After I did it the first time I felt so alive, so free and powerful. Rules lost their hold over me. When I shoot up [inject] I feel so independent, so wicked. It's the ultimate transgression, the unforgivable rebellion. The very 'badness' of shooting heroin is exactly why I didn't give it a second thought. ❞

Boredom leads some people to take drugs. When there is nothing to do, drugs may seem a tempting chance for some excitement.

Peer pressure

Young people are often pressured by friends to try drugs. They might feel isolated if they don't join in, or afraid that they will lose their friends if they don't go along with the gang.

Benji, from Northern Ireland, started taking ecstasy aged 14. He explains:

❝ I felt such pressure to be like the rest of them. You had to be big, be a man – you know, sure I can take this, or that, or whatever. I just went along with everything. Everyone was taking them and I started doing it too. We'd take them all the time. ❞

He had started smoking cannabis like this, too, but resisted pressure from his friends to take heroin.

"There are individuals who take psychoactive substances in the hope of developing themselves in some way... for [others] the destructive effects of drugs are an essential motive for taking them."

Professor Ted Goldberg, Stockholm University, Sweden.

In most parts of the world, drugs are readily available. Many people buy drugs on the streets or from friends.

"A young addict wants to prove that he is free; that he is a man, and he [may] harm the whole of society just to... prove that he exists."

Mahmoud Saleh, school anti-drugs advocate in Al-Orman, Egypt.

DO DRUGS MAKE YOU HAPPY?

How do drugs make you feel? Stimulants such as speed make people feel hyped up and full of energy. Depressants make them feel relaxed and uninhibited. And hallucinogens such as LSD produce strange, dream-like experiences.

Emotional escape

For people whose lives are unhappy in some way, drugs may provide a release from reality. Geoff takes ketamine, an anaesthetic used on animals that makes humans hallucinate (experience strange illusions). He first tried it while he was a soldier fighting in Korea:

" It was as if I found the key to a secret realm; as if I'd stepped through a magic door into heaven. "

Kribann, from South Africa, uses crack (a stimulant) to escape from feeling:

" Addicts take this stuff to obliterate the pain, not to feel good. We do it to feel nothing at all, to escape. "

Portia was a student in Bristol, UK, when she took heroin (a depressant) for eight months:

" Three seconds after pushing that needle into my veins I could have been God. Nothing in the world had ever compared to it. "

This woman in New York is smoking crack after injecting heroin. She may enjoy the feeling it creates, but combining drugs in this way is especially dangerous.

Some people take drugs at raves and festivals because they feel it gives them energy and helps them to enjoy themselves.

Ultimate high

Many people take drugs for the thrill of experiencing unfamiliar feelings. Craig lives in Canberra, Australia. He describes how he feels after injecting speed (a stimulant):

❝ Everyone feels immediately that the high from amphetamine is like nothing else. And the whole thing of giving yourself a shot is very sexual. After ten seconds, tops, you get this feeling creeping up the back of your neck. Your skin starts to fizz and prickle, and you really focus on it and wham! It's like your head explodes, and suddenly your mind has never been so alive, you're more awake than you've ever been in your life. Then the rush comes – it zaps into your head and your head is floating. It's the best feeling on earth. ❞

"I perceived an uninterrupted stream of fantastic pictures, extraordinary shapes with intense, kaleidoscopic play of colours. After some two hours this condition fades away."

Dr Albert Hoffman, inventor of LSD, after taking the new drug in 1943.

HOW BAD CAN DRUGS MAKE YOU FEEL?

Drugs don't always make you feel good. It's possible to have a bad experience taking them, especially if the drugs are contaminated with other substances.

Bad trips

A trip is a realistic vision or experience produced by a hallucinogenic drug. On a trip, people feel or see things that are not real but seem very real. On a bad trip, these can be terrifying, but it is impossible to escape or end the trip. Some people have flashbacks of a bad trip even many years later. Carrie, from Eire, had a bad trip after taking magic mushrooms:

" I felt like I was imagined by someone else and when they stopped thinking about me, I would just stop existing. "

Daniel is a Canadian artist. He takes hallucinogens to achieve spiritual visions. He describes what he saw on a bad trip:

" It was very dark, like hell. I screamed and screamed.... I knew I was stuck there for eternity – it was terrible. "

Kirsty had a bad experience with ketamine:

" I thought I'd never escape this nightmare, that I was slowly and painfully dying, but I wouldn't die – I'd continue to suffer for ever. "

Suffering the ill effects of drugs is usually a lonely and desperate experience.

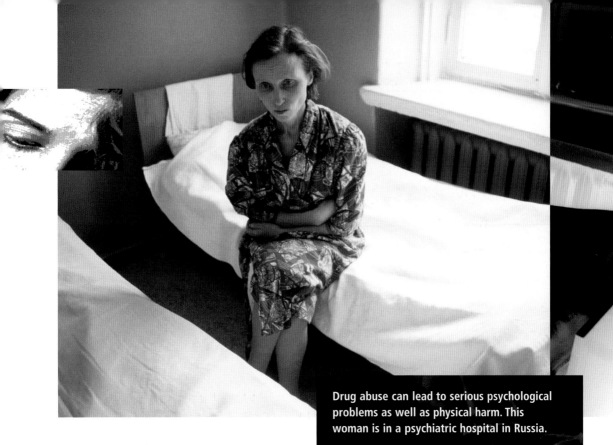

Drug abuse can lead to serious psychological problems as well as physical harm. This woman is in a psychiatric hospital in Russia.

Vicious circles

When the drugs wear off, bad feelings can be overwhelming. This often drives people to take more drugs. Craig, the speed-user from Canberra (see page 9), explains what happens when the effects of his fix fade:

❝ The amphetamine starts to wear off. You're wide awake and you can't sleep. It's the worst feeling in the world.... Suddenly, nothing in the world is right. You feel like all you want to do is cry and cry, desperately, but usually you can't. Your skin feels all spiky and prickly, you're agitated, hot and cold at the same time, having cold sweats and shaking, stuff like that.... You feel as if you've been staked out for the ants or chained up and beaten for days. The only way to be rid of it is to take more. ❞

"...she was no longer Mrs R [someone I knew], but rather a malevolent, insidious witch with a coloured mask. A demon had invaded me, had taken possession of my body, mind and soul. I jumped up and screamed, trying to free myself from him.... The substance with which I had wanted to experiment had vanquished me."

Dr Albert Hoffman, inventor of LSD, after taking the new drug in 1943.

AREN'T DRUGS SUPPOSED TO BE COOL?

Sometimes, the media and movies glamorise drug taking. Their air of alienation and rebellion can make drugs seem attractive, especially to young people who feel the world doesn't understand them.

Hard front

Often, drug taking is shown as 'hard' – something done by people who don't care what happens to them. Greg, a young American, boasts of using drugs to look tough:

❝ We were shooting dope in, like, a contest. One of us had to die. He'd shoot a half gram and then I'd have to shoot a gram. Next he'd shoot one-and-a half grams, and I'd have to shoot two.... We'd die before we'd back out. It was to the death. ❞

The characters may look carefree here, but in the film *Trainspotting*, abuse of drugs and alcohol leads to wrecked lives.

"I chose not to choose life. I chose somethin' else. And the reasons? There are no reasons. Who needs reasons when you've got heroin?"
Opening sequence of *Trainspotting*.

"The film celebrates the spirit of these young people, rather than the thing they do that will eventually destroy them.... It's not trying to celebrate heroin, it's celebrating a kind of spirit that exists in all of us before something like age, or a job – or heroin – crushes it."

Danny Boyle, director of *Trainspotting*.

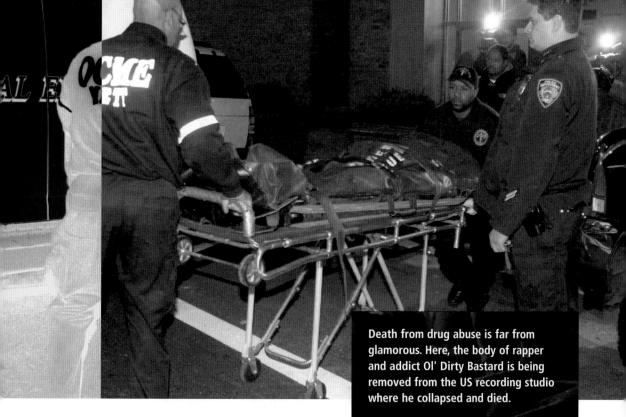

Death from drug abuse is far from glamorous. Here, the body of rapper and addict Ol' Dirty Bastard is being removed from the US recording studio where he collapsed and died.

Harsh reality

The reality of drug taking, for both celebrities and ordinary people, can be dependency, illness, ruined lives and relationships, and even death. Musician Pete Doherty has been a high-profile addict who at times spent £1,000 a day on heroin and crack cocaine. He has lost contracts with bands and had problems in his personal life because of his addiction. He denies that taking drugs is part of a glamorous way of life:

❝ What, you think I did it to feel glamorous? I don't know if taking drugs would make you feel glamorous, maybe the opposite. It might make you feel dingy or sordid. Or maybe for a split second you might feel elevated or glamorous, but I would never say drugs are glamorous or made me feel glamorous. ❞

WILL IT HURT TO TRY ONCE?

One reason people take drugs is precisely because they've been told they shouldn't. Because they are forbidden, drugs have an aura of mystery, rebellion and adventure that tempts people to give them a try.

Having a go

People may decide to try a drug out of sheer curiosity. They want to find out how it feels – they may not intend ever to take it again. Can it hurt if you take a drug only once?

Karl, from Germany, tried cannabis at the age of 12:

" I kept hearing about it, all my friends talked about doing it, and I was really curious so I just wanted to do it to find out. "

Tabitha explains that although she tried cannabis and speed at high school in Chicago, USA, she quickly gave up because she didn't like their effect:

" I tried pot and uppers for a while in high school, but I didn't like the way they made me feel. I prefer just being myself. "

An experiment with a joint is unlikely to lead to lasting harm – but can people trust themselves to stop once they've started using drugs?

Injecting heroin has many dangers, including addiction and disease.

Killer curiosity

Some drugs are very dangerous, even if taken only once. A single hit of crack may get you hooked. And without experience, people can take too much of a drug the first time.

Melissa and a friend bought a gram of cocaine and took it all at once (this would be enough for 12 lines). She describes how she felt:

" My whole face went numb; I was hyperventilating. It felt like my head was exploding and like my heart was going to explode. It was like my heart would escape from my body. I couldn't eat or sleep for two days. "

Tariq, from Islamabad in Pakistan, injected heroin for the first time with a friend. It had devastating effects:

" We got a needle and some stuff [heroin] from a guy we knew and took it for a laugh. Now I have HIV and I will get AIDS.... I just have to wait and see when. "

FIRST TIME

FIRST-TIME DRUG USERS IN USA

	1970	2001
COCAINE	288,000	1,167,000
HEROIN	85,000	162,000
CANNABIS	2,858,000	2,806,000
ECSTASY	255,000 (1976*)	1,786,000

(* no data available before this date)

SAMHSA, Office of Applied Studies, National Survey on Drug Use and Health, 2002 and 2003

WHY DON'T PEOPLE STOP?

People who use drugs to escape from misery often ignore the dangers of taking drugs, or think it is worth the risk because it gives them some relief.

Finding reasons

The feeling a drug induces may seem to fill a gap in someone's life. Cecily, aged 45, lives on a Native American reservation where most people are very poor. She says:

❝ Most people I know use OxyContin. They are like 'what the hell? I'm gonna stay high because I've got nothing.' We have nothing to lose, so why not? ❞

But there are other reasons. Jocelyn and her friends in Los Angeles, USA, have a very casual attitude to cocaine, which they use to help them stay slim:

❝ We're all doing it. We can lose weight really quickly. We take coke and don't eat for a day, sometimes two. I do it at least once a week. It's cheaper than the canteen, too! ❞

For some people, drugs provide a distraction from reality. These morphine addicts are injecting on the street in Multan, Pakistan.

Getting hooked

Long-term drug abuse can take away choices. People who become addicted feel compelled to carry on using drugs. Addiction may be physical – the body can't function without the drugs – or psychological, creating a desperate need for the sensations the drug produces.

Angie, from the Netherlands, used speed – a highly addictive drug – and struggled to overcome her addiction:

❝ If I stop using now I'll be very ill, and that's just from the detox [removal of poisons from the body]. There's no way I can learn to deal with everyday life again without chemicals, not without professional help. But I've found that getting the help I need isn't easy. They put me on Valium three months ago to shut me up. But now I'm addicted to that, too. ❞

Ndebele got very quickly hooked on a cold and flu medicine he buys over the counter in Zimbabwe. He says:

❝ I gave up everything else – I was totally obsessed with using it. All I cared about was getting high. ❞

Some addicts will try any types of pills they can find. They may have no idea what the drugs are or what the effects will be on their bodies.

ASIAN ADDICTS

INJECTING DRUG USERS IN PARTS OF ASIA

	NO. OF USERS	% OF POPULATION (2005)
RUSSIA	700,000	0.5%
UKRAINE	400,000+	0.8%
PAKISTAN	180,000	0.1%
INDIA	500,000+	0.05%

UN Office on Drugs and Crime, 2004

"Most experimental animals will press a lever to get an injection of cocaine, amphetamine, heroin, nicotine (sometimes) and alcohol. They will not press a lever for LSD, antihistamine, or many other drugs. This list of drugs... matches exactly the list of drugs that are viewed as clearly addictive in humans."
Cynthia Kuhn, Professor of Pharmacology, Duke Medical Center, North Carolina, USA.

ARE ANY DRUGS 'SAFE'?

Some drugs are considered fairly safe by many people. Cannabis and ecstasy are not usually associated with rapid addiction or bad after-effects. How safe are they really?

All drugs, including cigarettes and alcohol, could do long-term damage to your body. Some illegal drugs have a negative effect much more quickly.

Harmless fun?

Many people use drugs over an extended period of time without coming to obvious harm. They believe that moderate use of illegal drugs is no more dangerous than moderate drinking.

Poppy, from Australia, is a long-term user of cannabis. She is not worried about her habit:

❝ I've smoked weed for 35 years, which makes me pretty much an authority on the subject. I'm in perfect health and have all my mental faculties. I've achieved loads during the time I've been on weed. It's not addictive, like tobacco and alcohol, and you don't get withdrawal symptoms, like you do with crack. ❞

A bad reaction to a drug, or an overdose, can lead to the intensive care ward. Even drugs that are considered relatively 'safe' may have unpredictable effects.

Serious consequences

But things can go wrong. Cannabis use has been linked with schizophrenia and other mental illness, and skunk – extra-strong cannabis – often has serious effects on users. Ecstasy is not always safe, either.

Linnette, an actress living in Paris, France, used ecstasy. She says:

❝ It took only six months. At the start, I was living a normal life, pursuing my dream. By the end, I didn't give a damn about anything. The more I used, the further I retreated into a dark, lonely world. I could hardly sleep, but when I did I had nightmares. People say ecstasy is harmless, a happy drug. There's nothing happy about how it eroded my life. Ecstasy destroyed my dreams, cost me my friends, my apartment, my money and my mind. ❞

"Many hospitals in city areas have now seen at least one example of an ecstasy-related emergency and most units are now sensitive to this type of drug emergency."

Chris Jones, teacher of 'Critical Care Courses for Nurses', Edge Hill University College, Liverpool, UK.

"Ecstasy can, and does, kill unpredictably and there is no such thing as a safe dose."

David Blunkett, ex-Home Secretary, UK.

WHAT ARE DRUG ADDICTS LIKE?

The popular image of a junkie (drug addict) is of a desperate, ill-looking person, living in poverty and turning to crime or prostitution to finance their habit. Is it always like that?

Many drug addicts finance their habit through crime or prostitution, doing things they may otherwise never consider.

Self destruction

There are plenty of drug addicts who do fit the stereotype – who live from one hit to the next and are unable to function as part of normal society. Filip, from Amsterdam in the Netherlands, has had friends who have died from heroin abuse. He uses ecstasy and cannabis himself, but won't use heroin. He says:

" I've seen what heroin can do to you and I don't want to go there. I've got this friend, he's a proper heroin addict, a real junkie. He's injecting it into his neck, into his groin, even in his head. Arms and legs – they're useless. He looks anywhere he can find a vein that's still usable and he'll inject there. That's not the way I want to be. No way. "

Self control?

But many people keep their drug use under control or hidden. They may function normally much of the time. Ian, a doctor from Scotland, says:

❝ I've had many patients who were addicts, but held down a job or got qualifications. In some cases, not even their closest family knew about their addiction... your local drug addicts may not be the dejected beggars or the muggers with tracks up their arms – they might be serving you in a shop, sorting out your divorce papers, or arranging your insurance. ❞

A lot of drug users are indistinguishable from the rest of the population – even their own families may be unaware that they are users.

IS THERE A SLIPPERY SLOPE?

Some drugs are more addictive than others. Crack, ketamine, speed and heroin are highly addictive. A drug such as cocaine, which is not physically addictive, can still be strongly psychologically addictive. How do people become hooked?

Wanting more

Once a person is in the habit of taking a drug, the desire or 'need' for more can become overwhelming. Moussa is an Algerian man living in Belgium. He describes how he gradually became addicted to ecstasy tablets, which are not usually considered addictive:

❝ It just started getting harder and harder to take just one. You take one, and you take another one. After a couple of months, two's not enough. You're taking four, five, six. That's it, you just can't stop taking them, more and more. Every Friday night, taking more. You have to take just one more each time, just to get the same effect as that glorious first time. ❞

Many people take drugs such as ecstasy when they go clubbing at weekends. They may never take other drugs, or take them at other times.

From bad to worse

Ecstasy and cannabis are often called 'gateway' drugs, meaning that if people take these they are likely to go on to take harder and more dangerous drugs. A cannabis dealer who also deals in hard drugs will try to move users on, too, as other drugs are more profitable.

Kieran believes that cannabis opened the door to other drugs for him. He explains why:

" Smoking my first joint broke down the mental barrier put there by everybody in authority – by parents, by school – that drugs are off limits. That joint showed me that drugs were within my reach, all drugs, even class A's ['hard' drugs]. It showed me that I might enjoy doing them and it put me with the kids who were doing the harder stuff. "

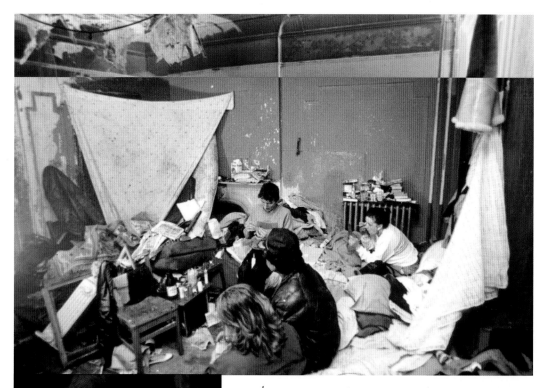

Abusers and addicts can end up in truly miserable conditions, like this crack house in New York, USA.

"There's no concrete evidence that cannabis is the 'gateway drug'. Tobacco is the gateway drug for most heavy drug users."
Dr Miriam Stoppard, UK.

HARD FACTS

● 95% of people who use hard drugs first used cannabis.

● 95% of people who use cannabis don't move on to hard drugs.

● Heroin users have a 1 in 3 chance of becoming addicted.

HOW CAN PEOPLE AFFORD DRUGS?

Drugs can be extremely expensive – taking heroin can cost £100 a day, and crack can cost £200 a day. It's easy to see how celebrities can afford a drug habit, but what about ordinary people?

Desperate measures

Many people turn to crime and prostitution to get the money to buy drugs. Leroy, who lives in Denmark, explains:

" Getting the money can be awful. You can try some sob story to get state handouts, or you can steal or you can work the streets. If you're gay, it's easy to sell sex for smack. "

Grace has been a prostitute in Scotland since a pimp lured her from a children's home and gave her heroin:

" I started when I was 12. I can turn ten tricks [have sex with ten clients] in half a day, and that keeps me sorted for a while. "

Addicts can lose everything, and end up begging on the street. Even the money they get from begging may go towards buying more drugs.

Money no object

Users with well-paid jobs can afford to feed a drug habit more safely. Charles, in Sydney, Australia, explains:

❝ All the people I did smack with were well educated. We had good jobs in the media, advertising, the stock market. Most of us had been using for years. No one ever needed to steal or hurt anyone else. We could pay and we had it under control. ❞

Being able to afford clean drugs, and being able to afford enough to smoke rather than inject, kept Charles safe, he believes:

❝ If you smoke heroin, you can manage the dose and you don't OD. But you need more to get the same high if you smoke than if you shoot up. It's too expensive for poor junkies. ❞

In some industries, including high fashion, film and the media, drug use is common and often quite open.

WHAT COST?

PRICES OF DRUGS IN THE UK, 2005

CANNABIS	**£2 a gram (enough for 2 joints)**
COCAINE	**£40–60 a gram (about 12 lines)**
CRACK	**£12–£20 a rock (a small chunk of powdered purified cocaine)**
ECSTASY	**£7–10 a tablet**
HEROIN	**£35 a gram (about 5 shots)**
LSD	**£1–£5 a tab**
SPEED	**£8–£12 a wrap (powder wrapped in a twist of paper or plastic)**

"A line of cocaine is now the same price as a cup of coffee bought from [a high street coffee outlet]. That probably says more about the price of cocaine than about the price of coffee..."

Nigel Evans, House of Commons, 2005, debating Drugs (Sentencing and Commission of Inquiry) Bill.

WHO DEALS IN DRUGS?

The worldwide trade in bringing drugs to drug users is worth billions of pounds. Millionaire gangsters mastermind huge shipments of cocaine from Colombia, while the drugs are distributed by dealers on the streets. Why do people work in the drugs trade?

Danger-junkies

The risky nature of the drugs trade can hold great appeal for some people. Polly, from Canada, became involved in drugs dealing in a fairly small way. It gave her money for heroin – but she also found the experience exciting:

> " Caz and I were small-time money launderers. It doesn't sound much, but we were so excited about it – it was so illegal and dangerous.... I carried about US$100,000 each time.... I'd tape packs of $100 and $50 bills around my legs and my stomach, then pull on baggy pants... the rush when I went through security at the airport was unbelievable. "

Drug deals often take place on the street where it's easy to run away if the police come.

Cocaine baron Lincoln White enjoyed an extravagant lifestyle before his arrest and imprisonment in 2004.

Around 80 per cent of the world's ecstasy comes from the Netherlands, where hundreds of millions of tablets are made every year.

BIG MONEY

PROFIT ON ECSTASY DEALING IN EUROPEAN COUNTRIES (US$ PER TABLET)

NETHERLANDS	$6–10
BELGIUM	$6–10
ITALY	$21–25
SCANDINAVIA	$5–12
UK	$14–15
IRELAND	$9
SPAIN	$2.75–14

Craving cash

Other people deal drugs for the money, whether they're earning millions from running an international operation, or just making cash for DVDs and their own drugs. Moving drugs around and selling them on is called trafficking. Boriqua lives in Brazil. She sells only to friends. She describes how she began dealing:

❝ I started on dope when I was 14. To start with, I'd give extra to friends. Then they started paying me. I don't deal full time – just for extra cash. ❞

Really successful dealers are rarely users. Instead, they make a fortune from master-minding the smuggling and distribution of drugs.

Doug, a dealer in Los Angeles, makes US$100,000 a year bringing pot from Mexico. He says:

❝ I was shooting up before I got into this business, and I would never be so successful if I were still on heroin. Every dealer I've known who became a junkie lost everything. ❞

HOW ARE DRUGS LINKED TO CRIME?

We are used to the idea that drugs and crime are linked. We are told that pirate videos finance drug dealing and that drug dealing funds terrorism. How does drug crime affect individuals?

Petty thieves

Drug-related crime ranges from petty theft by junkies to large-scale organised crime. Stuart, from Brisbane, Australia, talks about his brother, who is addicted to heroin and steals to buy drugs:

" He can't hold down a job. He steals from us and from his friends. He lives on the streets now, begging and stealing to get his next fix. He just lives for the drug. We've given up hope. Every time the phone rings I turn cold with fear – I'm sure it's the call to tell me he's died. I'm trying to cut him out of my heart – I can't bear to love him any more. **"**

This woman drug user has resorted to teaching her son how to deal in drugs on the street.

Opium farmers in Mexico defend their territories and trades with guns. Their opium is made into heroin and sold outside Mexico.

CRIME FIGURES

- In the UK, the cost of drug-related crime is around £20 billion a year.

- Of the 850,000 people in prison in Russia, around one-quarter committed drug-related crimes.

- According to the United Nations, the worldwide drugs trade is worth US$400 billion a year – the value of all Canada's exports (sales to other countries) in a year.

- In the year 2002–03, drug possession and trafficking offences in London, UK, rose by 27%.

Big business

Because there is so much money to be made from the drugs trade, it is riddled with corruption. Protection rackets (demanding money in return for refraining from violence) and violent crime characterise drug dealing in cities. In the developing countries where drugs are grown, violent groups fight over lucrative farms.

Pablo, a peasant farm worker near Bogota, Colombia, describes a massacre on his local coca plantation by a rival drug controller (coca is the main ingredient in cocaine):

" They tied us up and threw us on the floor like dogs and shot us. I was shot twice. I pretended to be dead so they would leave me alone – 34 people died. We are just poor peasants. We don't care who owns the farm, we only care about having work. **"**

WHAT IS DRUG SMUGGLING?

Many drugs come from plants grown in Asia or in South America and are smuggled over international borders. Some countries have a death penalty for drug smuggling – so why do it?

Minor mules

Smugglers are usually 'mules' – people paid to carry drugs. Porota was caught smuggling drugs from Colombia to the UK. She was sentenced to eight years in prison. She explains what happened:

❝ I carried drugs because I had no help supporting my children and things were very difficult for us.... These people trained me... by getting me to swallow things like grapes. I had to swallow them without chewing. When the time came, I carried the drugs in my stomach. Would I ever carry drugs again? No, no, no. No. Never. If I could turn the clock back, I would not do it. ❞

Smuggling drugs by hiding them inside the body – in packets that are swallowed or hidden in body orifices – is very dangerous. The packets can burst and poison the carrier.

In 2004, Australian Schapelle Corby was sentenced to 20 years in prison for smuggling marijuana into Indonesia.

DEATH PENALTY

Countries that may impose a death penalty for people caught smuggling drugs include: Brunei, China, Cuba, India, Indonesia, Iran, Laos, Malaysia, Mauritius, Myanmar, Oman, Russia, Philippines, Saudi Arabia, Singapore, Sri Lanka, Sudan, Syria, Thailand, United Arab Emirates and Vietnam.

These plastic bags, containing a total of 750kg of opium, were seized by police in Kabul, Afghanistan, in 2005.

Drug barons

The people behind drug smuggling deals are criminals intent on making money – and they make a great deal of money.

Roy, a 'drug baron', was imprisoned after an US$87 million haul went wrong. He says:

“ The big guys, like me, we don't usually get caught. The mules don't know who they're working for. I'll do my time, but when I'm out – I'll only have to do nine years of my twelve – there's still $70 million waiting for me. I don't need to go back to doing deals. They took $15 million, but they never found the rest – and when I've served my time, there's nothing at all they can do about it. ”

Ojide Ikubo, from Nigeria, was jailed in 1988 for drug trafficking:

“ I travelled all over the world trading in all sorts of drugs – cocaine, heroin, marijuana – you name it. When you are successful and get your dollars, it's like winning a lottery. ”

"We've been working our socks off for years, seizing more and more hard drugs; bringing more and more people to court. But... all this effort has had absolutely no effect on drug availability... we've been failing for the last 25 years."
UK customs officer, 2001.

SHOULD DRUGS BE LEGALISED?

In some places, such as Portugal, using cannabis is legal. In others, such as Saudi Arabia, even alcohol is illegal. Should certain drugs be against the law, or not?

Alcohol is a legal drug, but people still use it at dangerous levels. This man, unconscious after drinking too much, needs emergency treatment.

Ban them

Many people believe that legalising drugs has dangerous implications. For them, it seems obvious that drugs that can be very harmful should be illegal. Peter, in Belgium, says:

" Going soft on drugs will just encourage abuse and increase addiction. If we take away the drug dealers' market, they'll just come up with something even worse to hook people. What are we going to do? Legalise any kind of rubbish that comes on the market? "

Carol, from Australia, has a young son whose friends take drugs. She says:

" It's hard to tell kids something's wrong if it's legal. Being scared of getting caught, of the legal consequences, it does stop some kids taking stuff. "

"The fact that cannabis is relatively easy to obtain in coffee shops has not resulted in a greater increase in use than in other countries."

Trimbos Institute (national knowledge institute for mental health care, addiction care and social work), Utrecht, the Netherlands.

There is a lot of popular support for the legalisation of cannabis, as shown by this march through London, UK.

Allow them

Many people believe that drugs should be legalised. They say that a clean, lawful supply would keep users safe from dishonest dealers and contaminated drugs and reduce the large-scale crime involved in the drugs trade.

Fulton's son died after taking contaminated heroin. He believes drugs should be legalised, so that they can be properly controlled. He says:

❝ What we have at the moment is a free-for-all, where criminals are in charge of supply and what goes into drugs.... You can legalise and regulate the supply, as you do with other drugs such as alcohol and tobacco, or you can leave it in the hands of crime.... If there had been a controlled environment for my son to take his heroin, and it had been supplied legally, he would still be alive. ❞

DO YOU KNOW WHAT YOU'RE TAKING?

Drug dealers are out to make as much money as possible, and drugs are expensive. Some may mix, or 'cut', the drugs they sell with other substances. The contaminants can be more dangerous than the drugs.

Ecstasy tablets are often brightly coloured and stamped with fun logos to make them look appealing to young people.

Dirty drugs

Some contaminants, such as flour or plaster, are added to make a drug go further. Others are mixed in to change or increase the effects of the drug. Pal, from Hungary, had a bad time after taking dirty (contaminated) ecstasy. He has no idea what it was cut with. He says:

❝ There was a crack in the ground, and I thought I could see fire through it. Then it started oozing out and running over the ground towards me. I was terrified, gibbering – I thought I was being sucked into Hell. I'd taken E [ecstasy] before, but nothing like that had ever happened in the past. ❞

Drug users may encourage their friends to try different types or combinations of drugs, but who is responsible for the effects?

"The bottom line is the kids don't even know what they're taking."

Joe Ryan, undercover Narcotics Detective with the Miami-Dade Police Department, USA.

Killer cocktails

Some users get used to contaminated drugs, and then accidentally overdose when they get a clean supply. Some dealers mix drugs to increase users' dependence or to keep them loyal to the dealer. And some users will just try anything at all to see what will happen.

Hailey from Essex, UK, tried anything she could find, with no thought for its purity or even what it was. She says:

❝ I just didn't care – I'd take whatever I could get my hands on. If I found pills in someone's house, I'd take them. I'd buy from dealers, anything going – meth, heroin, crack, pills, K [ketamine]. It was like a grand, exciting experiment – oh, what will this do? After one concoction, I felt so ill I called an ambulance – I was that scared. ❞

"You're putting all your trust in a drug dealer to decide what you're going to put into your body. If they can cut the product... with something else to enhance [quantity], do you really think they're concerned with quality control?"

Staff Sergeant James Templeton, police drug control section, Edmonton, Canada.

VICTIM OR VILLAIN?

People start to take illegal drugs of their own free will, and often they turn to crime to continue taking. Should we treat them as criminals, or as victims of their own habits and of drug dealers?

Pure criminals

Many non-drug users say that those who take illegal substances are breaking the law outright. Alistair, from Vancouver, Canada, voices a common view that addicts should be punished:

❝ Smackheads are, by definition, criminals. They buy illegal narcotics. They use some. Most likely, then, they churn up the rest with a load of rubbish and sell it on to some other smackhead. They steal from their families, they pimp and prostitute, they cheat the welfare system. Of course they're criminals. And if they're locked up, they get a chance to come clean. So why not? They're criminals – treat them as such. ❞

Australian police arrest a man during a crackdown on drugs in Sydney, Australia, in 2004.

Innocent prey

But people who abuse drugs don't set out to become addicts. They may be victims themselves – of their own addiction, as well as of the drug dealers who exploit their vulnerability.

Matt started on cannabis, but soon moved on to LSD and then opium. He finally gave up when his father threatened to hand him over to the police if he didn't enter a detox clinic. He says of addiction:

❝ It's a disease, an illness. An addict is a person who is sick and people should do whatever they can to help that person get clean. An addict can't come clean alone. That's why we have meetings and chemical dependency therapists, and that's what friends are for. ❞

Should we feel sympathy for drug addicts, such as these sufferers in a rehabilitation centre in Vietnam?

"The government will not succeed in addressing this problem until it sees drug use more as a public health problem rather than just a criminal one."
Roger Howard, Chief Executive of Drugscope, UK.

"Strict criminal prosecution of dealers and organised crime groups [is essential]. But no less important [are] medical and social support for people who use drugs."
Alexander Zhukov, deputy prime minister of Russia.

WHOSE BODY IS IT ANYWAY?

Drug users often feel it's up to them what they do with their own body and they resent relatives, health professionals and the government telling them what to do. Are they right?

Personal choice?

Many drug users feel their actions are affecting no one else. Carson, from St Louis, USA, believes that he should be free to make the choice to take a risk with his health if he wants to:

" If I choose to take ecstasy on the weekend and I harm no one while doing it, why is it wrong? No victim, no crime in my opinion. I know the dangers and I know they are slight and I choose to take it anyway. It's nobody's business but mine. The people who have never taken drugs seem to preach to others about them. "

Carson's casual use of ecstasy may have no impact on others. But it's not the same for everyone. Many people are destroyed by drugs, wrecking their families' lives too.

"It's my life, I can do what the hell I want with it, and you can say that's an expression of existentialist 21st-century despair or you could say that it's an exciting discovery of a right."
Paddy Screecher, team leader of the Hungerford Drug Project (antidote service for drug users in North Islington, London, UK).

The parents of UK teenager Leah Betts at a press conference. Leah died after taking a single ecstasy tablet.

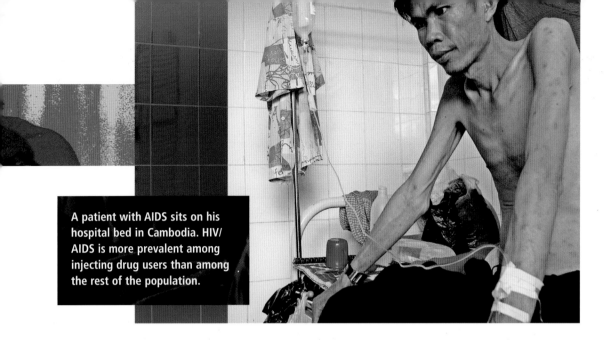

A patient with AIDS sits on his hospital bed in Cambodia. HIV/AIDS is more prevalent among injecting drug users than among the rest of the population.

Gradual devastation

Watching a loved one descend into addiction and refuse help is a devastating experience. Paulo's sister, Consuela, started shooting heroin as a teenager in Argentina. Paulo describes how he took a phone call from their brother:

❝ He said, 'Paulo, she's dead.' My soul left me at that moment. I was screaming and sobbing uncontrollably. I was in utter despair. There was nothing left for me. I will never forget that moment. I will never forgive myself for not being there the night she took the speedball, and how can I forgive her for taking it? No, my life is over, too. ❞

In addition, families may face the torture of seeing an injecting drug user developing HIV/AIDS or other diseases carried in the blood, such as hepatitis. HIV is passed from person to person in body fluids, and is common amongst drug users who share needles.

COSTLY PROBLEM

COSTS CREATED BY DRUG ABUSE IN THE USA (US$)

ANTI-DRUG PROGRAMMES	$19.2 billion	2001
POLICING, PROSECUTION AND IMPRISONMENT OF DRUG OFFENDERS	$30 billion	2001
KEEPING DRUGS OUT OF THE COUNTRY	$3.6 billion	2004
HEALTHCARE	$15.8 billion	2002
LOST PRODUCTIVITY (WORK NOT DONE BECAUSE OF DRUG ABUSE)	$128.6 billion	2002
DRUG USERS' SPENDING ON DRUGS	$40–50 billion	[estimate]

CAN FAMILIES HELP?

Drug addiction is hard to conceal – but some people do manage to hide it, even from their families. Others experience personality changes that are impossible for those close to them to ignore or understand. What impact does this have?

Drug addicts may alienate or reject their families to the extent that they end up homeless.

Offering support

Family relationships regularly break down because of a drug user's behaviour. Relatives suffer stress and anxiety, many fearing their loved one will automatically die. Drug abusers are often involved in crime, and frequently steal from their families.

Relatives may try to help, but addicts often refuse it. Annette, from Wellington, New Zealand, describes finding out that her son was addicted:

He was 18 when one of his friends told me he was smoking heroin. The bottom fell out of my world. I was sure he would die. But when I confronted him about it, he denied it. I was frantic.

Vitalik, a recovering addict who lives in Moscow, Russia, says:

An addict is in denial, he won't say there's a problem. He won't do anything until he sees he's hit rock bottom and there's nowhere else to go.

Strong relationships with a loving family increase an addict's chances of returning to a normal life without drugs.

Making a difference

Some families do help, though it is hard. Andrew was abusing many different drugs and had made lots of attempts to give up. It was his uncle who turned things around for him:

❝ He told me about losing his step-daughter, Fiona, to heroin. At the end, he put his hand on my shoulder and said, 'Throw away your drugs and make up with your girlfriend. Take your life back, day by day. Don't let this stuff kill you like it killed Fiona.' There were tears on his cheeks. I realised there was no easy way. I flushed 200 pills down his toilet. On the train home, I cried. After 22 years, I was finally going to be free. ❞

"Once they stop... taking drugs, their lives begin to open up again. In that opening process, they must have other people. Relationships are the only things that can fill that emptiness."

Babette Wise, Director, Alcohol & Drug Abuse Clinic, Georgetown University Hospital, USA.

IS THERE A WAY OUT?

What if you're already taking drugs and you can't handle it? It's never too late to give up, but quitting drugs is rarely easy. How do people escape from addiction?

Right company

To give up drugs, people need supportive family and friends. They often have to stop seeing friends who still take drugs. Genevieve from Toulouse, France, describes the panic other users feel when they see friends giving up:

" How does the junkie feel about the friend who's kicked and is really cool, taking steps towards recovery? She hates that person's guts. She's furious and envious that the friend can get out and she can't. And she panics. She can't bear the thought of being alone. She needs you to keep taking. "

Genevieve didn't escape. She has since died of an overdose of barbiturates.

Group therapy at clinics in hospitals and prisons often helps addicts to come to terms with their problems and begin the journey to recovery.

Community projects, such as this school art demonstration, can help to get the anti-drug message across to people who may not listen to authority figures.

HEROIN HORROR

- 1–2% of heroin addicts die each year of overdose, suicide, complications of drug-induced accidents and disease.

- In communities with HIV/AIDS as a significant problem, 3–4% of heroin addicts die each year.

- Taking 30 milligrams of pure heroin a day, addiction takes as little as 2–3 weeks.

Breaking free

But people can and do escape from drugs. Many get help from rehabilitation clinics ('rehab') – places that help them to come off drugs slowly, with medical help and counselling in a supportive and controlled environment. Often, rehab and education programmes in prison help drug abusers.

Craig, from New South Wales, Australia, had been abandoned by his family but he was helped by a drug programme in prison. He says:

" They shut you in your room and there's nothing much to do but think. I looked at the drugs info and I got thinking 'this is what it does to these people. What about me? Is it doing that to me? Or do I think I'm different, but I'm not really?' And I got help. I thank God I got caught and was put in here. I know now I'm not going to take drugs again. I've turned the corner, and I've got too much to lose. "

TIMELINE

4000 BC Inhabitants of Sumeria (present-day Iraq) use poppies, the source of opium, as a drug.

3000 BC Inhabitants of the Andes mountains in South America chew coca leaves, the source of cocaine.

1000 BC Mediterranean opium, used in religious rites in ancient Greece, is the first known drug used in Europe.

AD 1527 Opium is re-introduced to Europe by Paracelsus in the form of laudanum, a mixture of opium and alcohol.

1606 The first ship is chartered to bring opium from India to England.

1793 The British East India Company imposes a monopoly on opium production: Indian growers have to sell their opium to Britain.

1800 Napoleon's army brings hashish (cannabis resin) to Europe from Egypt.

1805 Morphine is isolated from opium in Germany; it becomes commercially available in 1821.

1839–42 The first opium war between the UK and China; Britain ran an illegal trade, bringing large quantities of opium from India to China where the drug was banned in 1836.

1850s Immigrant Chinese workers bring opium smoking to the USA.

1850s The hypodermic needle is invented.

1855 Purified cocaine is extracted from coca leaves in Germany. The technique is perfected in Austria and cocaine becomes commercially available from the 1880s.

1868 The Pharmacy Act (UK) is the first law to try to regulate drugs.

1870 An article published in a British medical journal first suggests that morphine may be addictive.

1874 Heroin is invented in Germany and sold into the USA as a safe alternative for morphine addicts.

1875 The first laws against opium smoking are passed in San Francisco, USA. Opium is still legal in other forms – the law is aimed at the unpopular Chinese residents.

1912 The Hague Opium Convention is the first attempt at international control of the drugs trade.

1915 The first law prohibiting the use of marijuana is passed in Utah, USA.

1916 The possession, distribution and sale of opium and cocaine are made illegal in the UK under emergency war-time legislation.

1920 The Dangerous Drugs Act, USA and UK, restricts the use of heroin, morphine and opium.

1928 The possession of cannabis becomes illegal in the UK.

1938 LSD is first made in Switzerland.

1955 The USA introduces the death penalty for supply of heroin to anyone under 18 years of age.

1967 The 'summer of love' marks the peak of 1960s hippy culture which embraces the use of drugs, particularly cannabis and hallucinogens such as LSD and magic mushrooms.

1973 The Drug Enforcement Agency is formed in the USA to enforce anti-drugs legislation and tackle smuggling and dealing.

1979 Illegal drug use peaks in the USA with one in ten people using some form of drug on a regular basis.

mid-1980s The success of crack in the USA swamps anti-drug teams.

1980s The emergence of HIV/AIDS leads to needle exchange systems to try to curb the spread of the disease amongst intravenous drug users.

1998 The United Nations sets out its plan to eradicate drugs completely by 2008.

2004 Cannabis is reclassified as Class C (the least offensive) drug in UK law; possession for personal use is no longer usually prosecuted (but still illegal) as long as the offender is over 18.

GLOSSARY

acid Another name for LSD, a hallucinogen that became popular in the 1960s.

amphetamine Another name for speed.

barbiturates Highly addictive depressants or tranquilisers, in the form of pills or capsules.

cannabis The leaves of the marijuana plant, dried and smoked like tobacco.

class A [drugs] The most dangerous drugs, for which legal penalties for possessing or supplying are most harsh.

cocaine A very fast-acting stimulant – a white powder, usually sniffed into a nostril.

crack Very strong cocaine, sold as crystals.

depressant A drug that makes people feel relaxed.

detox (detoxification) The process of removing toxins and drugs from the body.

dope Cannabis, or drugs generally.

drug baron Someone who masterminds drug dealing or smuggling.

ecstasy The stimulant MDMA in tablet form, widely used at raves and parties.

hallucinations convincing illusions involving sight, sound, smell and touch.

hallucinogen A drug that produces hallucinations.

heroin A depressant, sold as a greyish or brown powder and injected or smoked; it is fast-acting and very addictive.

hit Taking a dose of a drug.

joint A cigarette made with cannabis.

ketamine A dangerous depressant, used as a horse tranquiliser; sometimes cut with ecstasy.

money laundering Moving criminally-acquired money into the mainstream economy.

mule A person paid to carry drugs over an international border.

mushrooms, magic mushrooms Fungus containing a natural hallucinogen.

nitrous oxide Gas inhaled for its depressant effect.

OxyContin A narcotic approved for use as a painkiller but frequently abused.

pot Another word for cannabis.

schizophrenia A mental disorder causing breakdown of the personality.

skunk A very strong form of cannabis.

smack Another name for heroin.

special K Another name for ketamine.

speed A powerful stimulant supplied as a white powder, usually inhaled or swallowed.

speedball A mixture of heroin and cocaine.

stimulant A drug that makes users energetic, excited and exhilarated.

trafficking Trading in illegal substances.

trip The experience of taking a drug, usually a hallucinogen.

uppers Another word for speed.

RESOURCES

Books

Fiction
Go Ask Alice, Anon (Arrow, 1991)
The diary of a girl who became hooked on LSD.

Junk by Melvin Burgess (Puffin, 1997)
A teen novel about two heroin addicts.
Suitable for age 12+.

Smack by Melvin Burgess (Avon Books, 2003)
A teen novel about drug use, set in the 1980s.
Suitable for age 12+.

Reference and non-fiction
Alex Does Drugs (**Bodymatters**) by Janine
Amos (Evans, 2009)
How a young person acquires and copes with
drug addiction.

Drugs (**Wise Guides**) by Anita Naik (Hodder,
2005)
Dealing with drugs, friends who take them, and
pressure to take them.

Drugs: The Truth (**Teenage Health Freak**) by
Aidan Macfarlane and Ann McPherson (Oxford
University Press, 2003)
 Answers to typical questions about drugs.

How to Stop Time: Heroin from A–Z by Ann
Marlowe (Virago, 1999)
A first-hand account of a woman's heroin
addiction.

Film
Maria Full of Grace, 2004, directed by
Joshua Marston (Certificate 15) The story of
a Colombian teenager who becomes a drug
mule to make money for her family.

Websites

www.bdp.org.uk
A site dedicated to preventing harm caused
by substance abuse, giving advice on safer
practices, cutting back and giving up drugs.

www.drugaware.com.au
A comprehensive Australian site on all kinds of
drugs and the implications of use and abuse.

www.drugscope.org.uk/dworld
Drugs information and personal stories,
especially for 11–14 year-olds.

www.abovetheinfluence.com
Advice and information on all aspects of drug
use and abuse, including how to get help if
your parents are abusing drugs.

www.need2know.co.uk
Health information for teenagers, covering all
aspects of physical and mental well-being
including drugs, alcohol, smoking and diet.

www.talktofrank.com/
Down-to-earth, factual information about
drugs, and how to get help to come off drugs.

www.youngaddaction.org.uk/
Information about drugs for young people,
and help for people who abuse drugs.

Phone helplines

National Drugs Helpline: 0800 776 600
Immediate help and advice about drugs.
You don't need to give your name and calls
are free.

Childline: 0800 1111
Immediate help with any problem, including
your own drug abuse or drug abuse in your
family. You don't need to give your name and
calls are free.

INDEX